Braddock

Legends & Lore

Marci Lynn McGuinness

Braddock Legends & Lore © Shore Publications, 2016

ISBN: 978-0-938833-58-1
Published by Shore Publications, Ohiopyle, PA
Produced in the United States of America.

Marci Lynn McGuinness' books are available at: www.ohiopyle.info and www.amazon.com. Contact the Author: shorepublications@yahoo.com www.facebook.com/LaurelHighlandLegends

Quoted References: The Journals of Christopher Gist and George Washington. "Tariff Andy" speech.

A big thanks to Debbie Smith Moore Konechny and Pat Americo for their interviews, photos and laughs.

Cover photograph by Rich Moel.

Braddock's Inn is located at:
3261 National Pike, Farmington, PA 15437
Contact: 724 329-5508, Web: www.braddocksinn.com

CONTENTS

Author Marci Lynn McGuinness with Braddock's Inn owners and
long-time friends, Rhonda and Fred Zeigler.
August 2016, Rainbow 7 Car Show, Braddock's Inn.

I dedicate this book to Rhonda and Fred Zeigler, who have
whipped Braddock's Inn and the Stone House into shape,
preserving our precious history and giving us wonderful
places to play and stay. When Fannie Ross decided to sell
the Stone House to them twenty years ago, she said to me, "I
like that man!" Fannie loved men, and she had faith that by
putting her beloved home in Fred's hands, good things
would happen. She knew. And so did the Dunhams when
they recently sold Braddock's after forty years of service.

AUTHOR'S NOTE

Braddock Legends & Lore is my 36th book. I am very excited to be fortunate enough to continue to preserve the area's entertaining history. I bring you stories of our early pioneers and today's entrepreneurs, and thank everyone who shared their knowledge, photographs and support.

General Edward Braddock was shot on July 9, 1755. (Two hundred years later, to the day, I was born.) He did not die that day. He suffered until July 13, when they buried him in the trail which became Braddock's Road.

Rough taverns and all sorts of inns sprang up and the National (Pike) Road was constructed from Braddock's Road in the early 1800's. It's construction prompted Braddock's self proclaimed killer to show road workers where the General was buried. If Tom Faucet, 92 at this time, knew a monument would be erected in the General's honor,I bet he would not have bothered revealing the secret grave. He was most likely bragging about shooting Braddock.

This book is a collection of information, excerpts, newspaper clips and photographs depicting the General's horrifying mishap, and the life and times of the Braddock Inn's legendary people.

Thanks for READING!
Marci Lynn McGuinness

Rainbow 7 Car Show, August 2016

Well over 100 vintage cars were on display for our pleasure. Rainbow 7 is in honor of our mountain's famous race car driver, L. J. Dennis of Markleysburg, PA. Rainbow 7 was his winning car. He still restores autos and sports that ornery grin.

Have YOUR EVENT on the Braddock Inn Grounds

724 329-5508

Visit Braddock's Grave, monument erected in 1913.

The newly remodeled and rocking Braddock's Restaurant, Bar/s (inside and covered patio), inn, party room, and ice cream parlor. These historical landmarks sit adjacent to one another on the National Pike, Farmington, PA .

Tom Faucet stands over General Edward Braddock after shooting the Englishman for killing his brother in 1755.

Illustration by Colby Love, excerpted from McGuinness' book, *Gone to Ohiopyle.* Available on Amazon, at Backyard Gardens in Ohiopyle and Pechin in Dunbar.

Legends of
General Edward Braddock ,
Tom Faucet and
Young George Washington

Legend 1

In 1750, today's southwestern Pennsylvania was Colonial
Virginia. It was sparsely populated with Delaware, Iroquois
and Shawnee Indians and the traders who sold to them. The
French came south from Canada, establishing forts and
trading posts. The English were coming from Virginia to
claim this same territory.

The Ohio Company, a group of land investors formed in
1747, received a 200,000 acre land grant from the King of
England. They were to distribute this land to 100 families,
and build a fort to protect the colony. Christopher Gist, a
young surveyor, was paid 150 pounds to cut a trail through
the Allegheny Mountains while investigating the area from
Wills Creek (Cumberland, Maryland) to Fort Redstone
(Brownsville, Pennsylvania). He wrote every detail of his trip
in a journal for Lt. Governor Dinwiddie and established
friendships with the Indians and tradesmen along the way.

Legend 2

"The Journal of Christopher Gist, 1750–1751" – From
Annals of Southwest Virginia, 1769–1800, published 1929
by Lewis P. Summers:

"For the Honorable Robert Dinwiddie, Esquire, Governor
and Commander of Virginia.
Instructions given to Mr. Christopher Gist on the 11th day
of September 1750, by the governor, who was part of the
Committee of the Ohio Company,

*You are to go out as soon as possible to the Westward of the
great Mountains, and carry with you such
a Number of men as you think necessary, in Order to
Search out and discover the Lands upon the river
Ohio, & other adjoining Branches of the Mississippi down
as low as the great Falls thereof; You are
particularly to observe the Ways and Passes thro all the
Mountains you cross, & take an exact account
of the Soil, Quality and Product of the Land, and the
Wilderness and Deepness of the Rivers, & the several
Falls belonging to them, together with the courses and
Bearings of the Rivers & Mountains as near as you
conveniently can: You are to observe what Nations of
Indians inhabit there, their strength & Numbers, who
they trade with, & what commodities they deal in.*

When you find a large quantity of good, level Land, such as
you think will suit the Company, You are
to Measure the Breadth of it, in three or four different
places, & take the Courses of the River & Mountains
on which it binds in order to judge the Quantity: You are to
fix the Beginning and Bounds in such a manner
that they may be easily found again by your description; the
nearer the Land lies, the better, provided it be
good & level, but we had rather go quite down the
Mississippi than to take mean, broken Land. After
finding a large body of good Level Land, you are not to stop
but proceed further, as low as the Falls of the
Ohio, that we may be informed of that Navigation; And You
are to take an exact account of all the large
Bodies of good level Land, in the same Manner as above
directed that the Company may better judge
when it will be most convenient for them to take their Land.
You are to note all the Bodies of Good Land as you go along,
though there is not sufficient Quantity for
the Company's Grant, but You need not be so particular in
the Measuration of that, as in the Larger Bodies
of Land.
You are to draw as good a Plan as you can of the Country
You pass thro: You are to take an exact and
Particular Journal of all Your Proceedings, and make a true
Report thereof to the Company."

Christopher Gist journeyed to Colonel Thomas Cresap's home in Oldtown, near Cumberland, Maryland. Cresap was part of the Ohio Company, as were two of George Washington's brothers. Cresap was a tradesman, fighter, trapper and land speculator. He was also a good friend of native Delaware Indian Chief Nemacolin.

When the Delaware Indian Chief Checochinican passed away in 1750, his son became Chief Nemacolin, overseeing 160 warriors and many women and children. Their home was near Uniontown, PA, but they moved close to Fort Redstone at this time.

"We love this land Ohio Pile where we catch many fish and hunting feeds our families. We go today. Move to flat land. Our hunters will travel to the white frothy river, the Youghiogheny. It is my father's last wish to take our families to safer land," said the chief.

Note: These legends are an excerpt from McGuinness' book, *Gone to Ohiopyle.*

Legend 3

Thomas Cresap and Chief Nemacolin grew up together as neighbors and friends in eastern Pennsylvania. In 1752, Cresap asked his lifelong friend to help blaze the trail over the mountains because he would know the best route. The Indians followed old buffalo and elk herd trails while hunting and moving their tribes. Chief Nemacolin agreed and traveled with his sons to Oldtown, Maryland to assist Cresap and Gist in mapping out the old Indian trail. In 1752, Chief Nemacolin led the party through the rough Allegheny Mountains, cutting thousands of tomahawk markings into trees that needed cut away for "Nemacolin's Trail." When the men arrived back at Nemacolin's village near Fort Redstone, Chief Nemacolin's son, Lanocano, asked his father's permission to return with Cresap to live near his family. He was best friends with Daniel Cresap, Thomas' eldest son. He did move, taking his young family and his brother to Oldtown. Cresap renamed Lonacona, George Washington Cresap, to protect him from white prejudice and violence. Both Lonaconing, Maryland and Georges Creek were named for Lonacona. He died in 1790 (at the approximate age of 53) in the home of Daniel Cresap, and is buried in the Cresap Cemetery in Rawlings, Maryland. His daughter, Teresa, married William Workman of Mt. Savage, Maryland. Lonacona's brother, William, moved his family to Kerens, West Virginia.

Robert Dinwiddie was appointed Lieutenant Governor of Virginia, England's largest colony, taking office on July 4, 1751. As Lieutenant Governor, Dinwiddie was a persistent advocate of British expansion into the west. He sought out the assistance of the Indians and other British colonies in their goals to push back the French from the upper Ohio area. He fought the legislature to receive defence funds, and approved of the use of armed forces in place of the less reliable militia.

George Washington's elder half brother and mentor, Lawrence, died in 1752. Shortly thereafter, George inherited Mount Vernon. He was a county surveyor, and had spent much time with Lawrence among military men. He took Lawrence's place in the Virginia militia, receiving the commission of Major. This was our first President's first step in his military career. In 1753, he was 21. Dinwiddie sent young Washington to deliver a message to the Commander of the French on the Ohio River, demanding they leave the upper Ohio area.

Major George Washington, Christopher Gist, Indian interpreter John Davison and four men forged ahead from Wills Creek to Fort Duquesne (Pittsburgh). The Seneca Half King, Tanaghrisson, two other chiefs and one Indian hunter joined the party along the way.

Washington presented Dinwiddie's letter to French Commander Jacques Legardeur de Saint-Pierre at Fort Duquesne. The Commander was polite, but called a war council with his Generals.

Legend 4

Major George Washington wrote the details of the camp in his journal while awaiting the council's return. The site was almost surrounded by the south-west fork of French Creek. There were four houses on the perimeters and 100 men in addition to the many officers. One hundred and seventy pine canoes, 50 Witch Bark canoes, and many trees being blocked out for canoes, sat at the water's edge. The fort area contained bark and board-topped stables, barracks, smith's shops, a Chaplin's house, guard house, and doctor's lodgings. Eight cannons were mounted.

When the council returned, they offered Washington and his men provisions including liquor. They refused to let the Half King leave until the next day, promising him and his men guns if they would stay. Soon, Washington and Gist almost drowned in the ice-choked Allegheny River as they had to abandon their raft.

In 1754, Dinwiddie published Washington's 900-mile journey journal in Williamsburg and London, establishing an international reputation for the 24 year old man. Just a few months after his return from Fort Duquesne, Washington was made a Lieutenant Colonel. He was then dispatched with 150 men to widen Nemacolin's Trail and to reinforce Fort Redstone, using what force was needed to ward off the French. Christopher Gist joined the men on this expedition. Colonel Joshua Fry was to follow Washington's forces with heavy artillery and another 150 men, and to oversee the brigade.

The troops left Wills Creek in early April and travelled in heavy rain. On May 18, they reached the Youghiogheny River where the water was too high to cross. Indians and traders told young Washington that the mountains were too rugged to cut a road large enough to move heavy artillery.

He had the men carve a log canoe and paddled downstream while Lieutenant West, three soldiers and an Indian guide walked through the dense forest. They camped where the Youghiogheny and Cassellman Rivers meet Laurel Creek. George Washington named the spot "Turkey foot" because the three waterways formed the fowl's claw. This name stands today. When they continued on downstream, they met a trader who warned them of the rapid water ahead. Washington gave up the idea of transporting fire-power down the swift Youghiogheny River just upstream of Ohiopyle Falls.

Washington was pulled from the water saying, *The water becomes so rapid as to oblige us to come ashore.*

He wrote in his journal to Joshua Fry, *The Youghiogheny will never be navigable.*

The men hiked 30 miles back to the troops (today's Youghiogheny Dam area) and continued west on Nemacolin's Trail to the Great Meadows in Farmington, PA.

Legend 5

On May 24, 1754, Lieutenant Colonel Washington and his troops arrived at the Great Meadows in Farmington. They were told the French were nearby, so they quickly organised their wagons into the natural entrenchments the land afforded. Washington was visited by his friend, the Seneca Half King Tanaghrisson, (who had been kidnapped by the French as a child and sold into slavery). The Half King urged him to attack immediately as the French camping close-by were hostile. They planned to raid that night.

Scouts were sent out to find the French's camp just a few miles away. Through a drenching spring downpour, Washington, 40 of his men, the Half King and his warriors, journeyed through the night. They found the camp at dawn. The French claim they were ambushed and the English claim the French opened fire on them as they approached. Ten Frenchmen were killed including their leader, Joseph

Coulon Jumonville. Twenty one were injured. Many were scalped.

Jumonville was treated as a Prisoner of War by Washington, but as he was questioning the French leader, the Half King approached and sunk a tomahawk into Jumonville's skull. This action prompted the onslaught of the French and Indian War.

When Jumonville's half brother, Captain Coulon de Villiers, was told about the slaughter, he immediately planned his revenge. From May 30 to June 2, Washington and his men built a fort out of "necessity" as they knew the French would soon retaliate. On June 2, they held a religious service and the Half King returned with over 25 Indian families, fleeing from the French. Colonel Joshua Fry died on his way to the new fort. Young Washington was put in charge of the brigade.

Legend 6

On July 3, in the pouring rain, the French attacked "Fort Necessity" killing 30 English and wounding 70. Half of Washington's men were injured, sick or dead. His stock of ammunition was low and the gunpowder, wet. On July 4, Washington led his men from the fort after their surrender to the French, with drums playing and flags waving. They marched to Fort Cumberland, weak and beaten. Washington soon resigned his commission.

British statesman Horace Walpole called Jumonville's death the "Jumonville Affair" saying, *A volley fired by a young Virginian in the backwoods of America set the world on fire.*

Legend 7

In 1755, General Edward Braddock was sent by the King of England (in addition to Dinwiddie and the Ohio Company) to drive the French from the Ohio Country. Washington accompanied the army along Nemacolin's Trail as a volunteer aid. A dozen Indian scouts were leading 1200 British and colonial troops to Fort Duquesne (Pittsburgh), but their lack of supplies and training did not prepare them for this journey into battle.

They were ordered to widen Nemacolin's Trail to 12 feet along the way, building bridges where needed. They renamed the trail, Braddock's Road. Exhausted, they stopped at Fort Necessity. Many men were ill, including George Washington. Their flour had gotten soaked and the men were in need of provisions. Several hundred local soldiers and many women and children joined the regiment. Braddock took half of the troops to rush to Fort Duquesne. Legend has it that Braddock buried the payroll (gold!) along the Youghiogheny River at this time. Washington had repeatedly advised Braddock to fight "combat style" rather than in English formation, but the General refused.

Washington followed a day later, as he was very ill by now. Soon after, he and his men reached Braddock's army, (July 9, 1755). They were surprised in the woods by 300 Indians and 30 French soldiers. The Indians surrounded them on the trail at the Monongahela River and fired into them for two hours. They were packed on the narrow path, making it impossible to escape. Twenty-six British and American officers were killed, 37 wounded. Four hundred and thirty soldiers were killed, 385 wounded. Less then 30 French and Indians were killed, wounded unknown. General Braddock was mortally wounded.

Then the British *broke and ran*, said Washington, *as sheep before the hounds.*

Legend 8

Tom Faucet was a soldier from Shippensburg, PA fighting against the French on July 9, 1755. Years later, he ran at least one tavern on the National Road near Summit Mountain. He told this tale many ways through the decades, but he always insisted that he shot General Braddock. He claimed that the temperamental Braddock shot his brother,

Joseph Faucet, because he insisted on fighting "Indian" style (from behind trees) against the General's direct orders.

During this battle, the still-sick Washington attempted to rally the British soldiers, while having two horses shot out from under him, four bullet holes shot through his coat, and one through his hat. Washington served as leader while he and the survivors gathered up Braddock and marched back to Fort Necessity.

General Edward Braddock died at Fort Necessity on July 13, 1755. He was buried in Braddock's Road not far from the fort. George Washington led the burial service because the Chaplain had passed on. Washington then ordered the men to run over the grave with wagons and horses so the French and Indians could not find it and desecrate Braddock's remains.

We shall know how to fight them next time, were Braddock's reported last words to Washington.

Legend 9

In 1804, Tom Faucet was 92 years old. He several walked rough miles from his shanty on Kentuck Knob above Ohiopyle across the mountain to Farmington. A crew led by Wharton Township Road Supervisor Abraham Stewart, of Gibbon Glade, was cutting out the National Road. Andrew Stewart, 13, had gone to work with his father this day.

Faucet walked up and pointed out the spot where General Edward Braddock had been buried in 1755. The grave had been sought through the years, but went undetected until this time.

Abraham Stewart and his crew unearthed General Braddock's bones and a few British military coat buttons. They moved him off of the road, reburying him close-by.

Young Andrew Stewart soon put himself through law school and became District Attorney of Fayette County at the age of 29. In 1822, he distributed free watermelons while campaigning for Congress.

1822 – The same year Andrew Stewart won his first seat in Congress, he built the Fayette Springs Hotel (now known as the Stone House) on the National Road just west of Braddock's Grave. He was 30 years old and already starting to amass the 80,000 acres of Fayette County property he owned at his death. Stewart hired Colonel Cuthbert Wiggens to construct the popular inn that served the wealthy.

Just over one hundred years later, the Braddock Inn was built and in 1943, sold to a man named Andrew J. Stewart (98 years old on September 20, 2016, says they are no relation...coincidence?). See his recollections after this series of photographs and clippings...

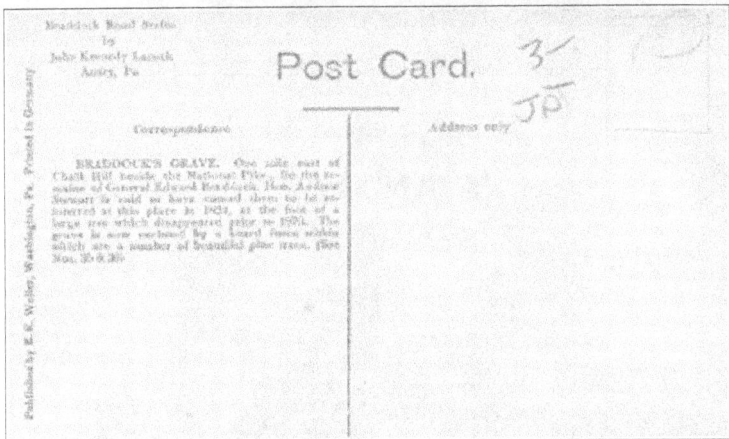

General Braddock's Grave, 1908 Postcard info:
BRADDOCK'S GRAVE. One mile east of Chalk Hill
beside the National Pike lie the remains of General
Edward Braddock. Hon. Andrew Stewart is said to
have caused them to be interred at this place in 1824
at the foot of a large tree that disappeared prior to
1870. The grave is now enclosed by a board fence
within which are a number of beautiful pine trees.

Braddock Park Inn, 1929

A few items from the local papers, 1929...

Tornado at Farmington

Connellsville, Pa., June 28.—A tornado which struck in the Farmington, Pa., section today apparently was limited to a small section, and no loss of life occurred, it was believed here this afternoon.

Communication lines between here and Farmington, 27 miles distant on the National Pike, were down, but reports were gained from nearby points.

The store of Charles Rush was unroofed and stock valued at $8,000 exposed to rain damage, it was reported.

The Cable service station was demolished, and Gwendolyn Cable, daughter of Roy Cable, owner, was

(Continued on Page 2)

FOR SALE

"Iron Age" Two-horse Potato Digger. Like new. Cheap. Inqutre Grace Rohlf, Farmington, Pa.
S 14 17 2t*-wky 1t

$655 PLYMOUTH

AND UPWARDS
F.O.B. DETROIT

New Lower Prices

A Triumph of Value Giving

Economy with Full-Size —Plymouth is the outstanding full-size car in this price class, giving room for five grown-ups, with real economy of operation;

Economy with safety — Plymouth's weatherproof hydraulic four-wheel brakes give instant stopping in any weather — another feature possessed by no other car near this price;

Economy with power — Plymouth's 45 h. p. engine assures typical Chrysler pick-up and getaway plus ability to maintain high average speeds with quiet smoothness;

Economy with modern engineering — Chrysler engineers designed Plymouth's modern high-compression L-head engine embodying such important improvements as aluminum alloy pistons, large main bearings, positive pressure-feed lubrication, rubber engine mountings and torque reaction neutralizer;

Plymouth Prices Effective December 20th — f. o. b. Detroit.

Coupe	$655	2-Door Sedan	$675
Roadster	675	De Luxe Coupe	695
(with rumble seat)		(with rumble seat)	
Touring	695	4-Door Sedan	695

Chrysler Motors' great cardinal principle in designing and building the Plymouth is to give the highest possible quality, the greatest possible value, dollar for dollar.

If you will compare the Plymouth, feature by feature, with the few other cars in the lowest-priced field, you will need no salesman to point out Plymouth's many superiorities.

Plymouth is winning on the score of greater dollar value — and you can prove that fact to yourself in far less time than it takes to tell you.

F. B. MILLER MOTOR SALES

28-30 West Fayette Street   Phone 510   Uniontown, Pa.
Associate Dealers
NEW SALEM, BROWNSVILLE, PT. MARION AND FARMINGTON, PA.

And a little 1930 news...

WASHINGTON'S SACRED GROUND

By M. M. HOPWOOD, Esq.

Historian General, National Organization of The Sons of the American Revolution. Historian of Fort Necessity Chapter, Sons of the American Revolution.

There were several distinguished Indians who were with Washington at Fort Necessity. Of these were: Tanacharison, the half-king of the Senacas, a friend of Washington's; Monacatootha, a chief of the Six Nations; Queen Aliquippa, and her son, and Shingiss, a Delaware chief and others friendly to the English. They took refuge at the fort, and some acted as scouts to watch the advance of the French and their Indian allies, as they marched on the fort.

After the surrender of Washington these Indians withdrew with him to Virginia, but soon after returned to Pennsylvania, and the half king died at Harris' Ferry, now Harrisburg, in 1754.

May 24th, 1754, Washington's little army reached Great Meadows, where the scouts reported the French army approaching, and the same evening he had this confirmed that the French were at Stewart's Crossing, only eighteen miles away. Thus warned, Washington began the construction of Fort Necessity and three days later he wrote: "We have with nature's assistance, made a good entrenchment, and by clearing the bushes out of these meadows, prepared a charming field for an encounter."

On the 27th of May, he again writes: "This morning Mr. Gist arrived from his place, where a detachment of fifty men were seen yesterday at noon, commanded by M. LaForce. He afterwards saw their tracks within five miles of our camp. I immediately detached seventy-five men in pursuit of them, who I hope will overtake them before they get to Redstone, where their canoes lie."

That night the half-king with some of his men, was in camp about six miles distant from the Great Meadows, and sent a messenger to Washington that, he had tracked the Jumonville party to their hiding place in an obscure ravine, surrounded by rocks. It was a dark and rainy night but Washington with forty men set out for the camp of the half-king, where he counseled with the Indian chief, and determined to attack the French. Early in the morning of May 28th they surprised the French in their camp, and in the skirmish that followed, Jumonville and others were killed, and La Force, Drouillon, two cadets and seventeen others made prisoners, and sent to Williamsburg, Virginia, where they were detained.

This skirmish in the night time, led up to the battle at Fort Necessity, and was the beginning of the French and Indian war.

Washington sent back for reinforcements and began to strengthen Fort Necessity by erecting palisades and otherwise protecting his little army against attack. June 9th Major Muse joined them with the balance of the Virginia troops. Washington hired horses to go back to Will's Creek (Cumberland) for more ammunition and provisions. June 10th Captain MacKay came up with his South Carolina company, but as he bore a King's commission he refused to receive orders from the Virginia Colonel. Rather than have any conflict of authority, Washington left MacKay at the fort, and with the Virginia troops, set out towards Redstone, building the road as he advanced. In two weeks he reached Gist's place, and here he detached seventy men, with orders to clear a road to the mouth of Redstone Creek. These men were in command of Captain Lewis. Another company under Captain Polson was sent out to do scout duty.

The French and Indians in the meantime were busy with preparations to attack Washington, and on the 28th left Fort Duquesne with five hundred French soldiers, augmented by about four hundred Indians, under command of de Villiers, a half brother of Jumonville. This army went up the Monongahela river to the mouth of Redstone Creek, using big canoes. From this point they hurried to Gist's plantation, which they found abandoned.

Learning of the approach of the French, Washington called in the men under Polson and Lewis, and began his retreat to Great Meadows, and greater strength was added to the fort, which was now called Necessity, as this defense had to be made there. The men had no bread for eight days and the milk cows had to be used for beef, without salt. At the fort they had some chopped flour, and provisions from the settlements sufficient to last them four or five days by using economy.

It rained all night July 2nd and the morning of the 3rd, a wounded scout came in, and reported the French and Indians, nearby and with great strength. Soon after the French opened fire on Washington's troops, at a distance of several hundred yards, where they were protected by the woods. The distance prevented any damage. In order to draw them away from their protection among the trees, Washington took a position in the open meadow outside the fort, but the French declined to leave their place of vantage. Washington then retired his men inside the fort, and for regular fighting followed until darkness settled over the scene.

DeVilliers, the French commandant asked for a parley which was refused. Again the French officer asked for a parley, which Washington granted on account of lack of ammunition and shortage of provisions. The French had no positive knowledge of the weakened condition of the English forces, except for a deserter who had fled to the French, and told them of the lack of food and ammunition which had failed to reach him. During the engagement July 3rd the French and Indians had killed and stolen his horses and cattle and thus made difficult his further retreat as well as defense; yet with all his handicaps he secured terms of surrender most honorable.

The articles of capitulation were drawn in the French language, with which Washington had no knowledge. He was allowed to retire without insult or outrage, and take with him baggage and supplies. The English colors were to be struck at daylight July 4th, and Washington's forces march out with colors flying, an drums beating. These were the terms of his surrender, and with the horses gone, the wounded and sick had to be carried all the way to Will's Creek on stretchers.

The French then took charge of the Fort and destroyed it on July 4th, 1754. Washington's loss was twelve killed and forty-three wounded. The French acknowledged three killed and seventeen wounded. After destroying Fort Necessity, the French hastily retired toward Fort Duquesne, as they were expecting reinforcements from Will's Creek to join the English army and felt they were unwilling to meet a force equal to or superior to their own, and they retired with such speed that they marched skirmishes after destroying the fort July 4th, and in two days had reached the mouth of Redstone Creek and taking their canoes immediately started for Fort Duquesne.

Fort Necessity

PUBLIC interest generally in re-creating Fort Necessity as a national shrine under federal administration should be expressed in support of the Sons of the American Revolution in an effort which takes tangible form tomorrow with the visit here of an assistant secretary of war to inspect the famous battle-ground.

It has always seemed to us that Fayette county has been more or less a "backward county" in the matter of memorializing its historic spots. We do not minimize what has been done.

But few counties anywhere in the nation have more right to recognition historically, have a more just demand upon the federal and state treasuries, more reason to unite in an aggressive co-operation that will bring about restoration or preservation of historic spots which are inextricably linked with the very foundation of American independence and progress.

1930

CITIZENS MUST BUY FORT NECESSITY IF IT'S TO BE PRESERVED

UNIONTOWN, Jan. 14.—To have Fort Necessity, the site of George Washington's first and only defeat, commemorated in a fitting manner ground will have to be purchased by patriotic citizens for a patriotic organization. The U. S. Government will not go to any expense of acquiring any land. These facts were made clear by Cononel H. L. Landers, Assistant Secretary of War, in charge of memorial parks who, with Congressman Samuel A. Kendall came here today for an inspection of the historic spot in the mountains near Farmington.

Colonel Landers said he considered the Fort Necessity matter of minor importance as compared with other historical sites which have been called to his attention within the last two and a half years. Colonel Landers indicated that he would make a recommendation to the War Department for a memorial, and the 200 acres including the historical scene surrounding Fort Necessity be purchased by outsiders.

The secretary said that between 3,000 and 4,000 requests similar to that from Uniontown had been made to his department. Including in the list he said was one from West Point, Mo., who claim that the battle which turned the tide in the Civil War was fought there.

The following letter from Harry Beeson, mailed simultaneously to Fayette county newspapers, contains an excellent suggestion for the commemoration of the 175th anniversary of the death of General Braddock, whose wayside grave in our own mountains is one of the historic spots of the community. We commend Mr. Beeson's suggestion heartily, appending his letter herewith:

During the spring and summer of 1755 American history was made that can never be effaced. The march of General Braddock across our mountains, his defeat, retreat and death will always stand out in world's history. As you will note this was just 175 years ago. For more than a year, our neighbor, the city of Braddock, has been preparing a mammoth celebration in commemoration of this event. That is attracting nation-wide attention.

Hadden's history tells us that General Braddock died the evening of Sunday, July 13, 1755, and was buried on Monday, the 14th, at or near the present site of his grave in our local hills. Strange to say, July 13, 1930, falls on Sunday, 175 years later. So far I have seen no notice of any arrangements being made by any of our local civic or patriotic bodies to celebrate this historic event. Why?

What would be more fitting, what would do more to draw attention to our great national highway and its historic surroundings? Why not a Sunday and Monday religious and patriotic celebration?, Why not invite that citizens of Braddock to make an automobile visit to Braddock's grave on this occasion as part of their own celebration, as well as all other nearby cities and towns?

I can think of nothing that would give our highway as much nation-wide publicity as something along this line. Let me add that Braddock's Grave and the site of Fort Necessity have never been properly marked to catch the eye of the approaching tourist. Many times have I been told why tourists passed those spots and did not know

what they were until too late.

The only reason the tourists are weaned away from our highway is because we are asleep. With a little effort from proper sources the Pike could be open to Brownsville and cemeted to the Summit before July 13.

Respectfully submitted,
HARRY BEESON.

Corrections to Errorgrams

(1) The Old Curiosity Shop was made famous by Charles Dickens, not Charles Lamb. (2) Shakespeare was born at Straford-on-Avon, not in London. (3) Curiosity is spelled incorrectly on the wall of the shop. (4) Three pounds is close to $15 instead of only $10 dollars. (5) The scrambled word is INERTIA.

Anniversary of Battle of Braddock to be Observed

Braddock, North Braddock and Rankin are scenes today of active preparations for the 175th anniversary observance, on July 8 and 9, of the battle, an outstanding event in the annals of pioneer days in Western Pennsylvania, in which General Braddock, leading his British and Colonial troops in an expedition against Fort Duquesne, was met on the banks of the Monongahela, ten miles from his goal, by the French and their Indian allies and was defeated, General Braddock being mortally wounded.

Historians have attached significance which proved disastrous in the wilderness.

National recognition has been given to the celebration by the authorization of a commemorative two-cent stamp and by the creation of a United States commission to participate in the event.

A heroic statue of George Washington, depicted as a young Colonial colonel when he took part in the battle, will be dedicated on a site near the center of the battle. Washington distinguished himself in the battle.

The statue, the work of Frank Vit-

Congressman Clyde Kelly of Braddock, left and Frank Vittor, sculptor, are shown in photo with model of statue of George Washington.

to the battle in that confidence was instilled in the colonist in their own mode of fighting as against the European method, which General Braddock insisted upon using against advice and

tor, Pittsburgh sculptor, will be used in designing the commemorative stamp.

The United States commission was created through the efforts of Con-

Clyde Smith lived nearby Braddock Inn and raced this car on Summit Mountain in the late 1920's and early 1930's.

Racing on Summit Mountain, 1940's.

Should the Uniontown Speedway Be Rebuilt?

In all circles, particularly the automotive, local discussion drifts at times to the question: "Should The Uniontown Speedway Be Rebuilt?" One thing is certain—from the standpoint of publicity for good old Uniontown few innovations have been brought forward that could equal it in ability to gather newspaper space in even the leading dailies of the country. And who can forget those "speedway day" crowds that thronged the city—leaving their trail of dollars with local merchants. And the thrill of the burning rubber as the gas demons ploughed their way 'round the boards. In all probability discussion on the Uniontown Speedway will be doubled Thursday, Friday and Saturday of this week, for Paramount is bringing to the State theater the first all-talking picture of the roaring track—"Burning Up," starring Richard Arlen and Mary Brian. Harry Hartz, 1926 champion of the A. A. A. acted as technical director for the production which, in addition to being the first speedway talkie, is also rated as one of the most entertaining pictures of the year.

Those Who Had a Part in the Construction of the First Uniontown Speedway . .

as well as the thousands who watched it during the course of construction and while the various races were in progress, will find added enjoyment at the State starting tomorrow. As a special feature in connection with the showings of "Burning Up" the management of Fayette's Foremost theater has brought from its film vaults original "movies" taken years ago at the Uniontown Speedway during construction and at several of the races. These "Bits From the Past" have been assembled into a prologue reel to "Burning Up" and will contain many surprises as well as dozens of laughs. Just imagine local movies made a decade ago! You may see yourself as you looked while watching a thrilling race at the speedway long ago! Scenes of the carpenters building the speedway; officials in charge of the construction; well-known the speedway; officials in charge of the construction; well-known Uniontown celebrities; thrilling accidents on the wooden saucer! All of them were caught by the lens of Charley Basley's camera —and are brought back to you from the past! A treat not to be missed in connection with the showings of the first speedway talkie, "Burning Up."

1930...FYI; the State Theater does not have the clips mentioned in this article. No one seems to. Marci McGuinness' books about the board track are available on Amazon. Her film TBA.

Clyde Smith and daughter, Audrey, at the Smith house near Braddock Inn, 1950's.

SCENE ON NATIONAL HIGHWAY FROM BRADDOCK'S MONUMENT, EAST OF UNIONTOWN, PA.

On the back of this postcard, it said:

Hello Edith,
All well. Your pad shipped today. Also box candy. Will write tonight.
Lots of love,
Dad and family

Addressed to: Mrs. Edith M. Smith, South Mountain, Franklin County, PA. Feb. 29, 1933

Contributor Debbie Smith Konechny grew up by Braddock's Inn, sneaked cigarettes, and smoked them on the Braddock's Grave steps with neighbors.

Braddock Inn Recollections

by former Braddock Inn Proprietor, Andrew J. Stewart,
who turned 98 years old 9/20/2016.

George Adele owned property on both sides of Route 40.
There were 30-some acres on the Braddock Inn side and
unknown acreage on the opposite side of the road, which is
now owned by the Sherry family.

George Adele may have owned an ice business in
Uniontown. He was also Secretary of the Brewers
Association, maybe 1930's.

George had Braddock Inn built in the late 1920's. It was a
two-story building with kitchen, bar, and eating area on the
first floor and four bedrooms and one bath on the second
floor.

George rented the building and grounds, but sold the
restaurant, bar, and gas pumps as a business.

About 1934, Donald and Ada Haas (Andrew Stewart's
mother and step-father) bought the business at Braddock's
Inn from a couple (probably first business owners) who had
not been successful there. After the sale closed, Donald and
Ada Haas learned that there were many debts to vendors
that they eventually paid off.

Donald and Ada had no liquor license for about a year, but Andrew remembers shots of whiskey being sold to people in the kitchen pantry! Eventually, having a liquor license helped make a profit. A beer cost 15 cents or 2 for 25 cents. "Poke me up a six-pack" was the expression used to order six beers in a paper bag (poke) to-go.

They served soup and sandwiches, had three covered picnic tables in the side yard, and four gas pumps to complete the business.

Two bedrooms on the second floor were sometimes rented to late night, winter travelers. Andrew remembers a couple from New York spending the night. Oh how Art Barclay, a colorful local, entertained everyone with his stories of bear hunting in Potter County. The couple said they could make a fortune if they could get Art on stage!

Another memorable local was Vic Holt who had a lumber business. He delighted in devising moneymaking schemes and suggested Donald Haas make a motor oil display with a can for 25 cents or 3 cans for $1.00. I don't think this went beyond the idea stage.

In 1943, Andrew and Madge Stewart bought the Braddock Park Inn business from Donald and Ada Haas, but cannot remember the amount of the sale. Andrew and Madge had a bar and served soup, sandwiches, ice cream, Popsicles and gasoline.

One summer they offered an outdoor movie each week with people sitting on blankets in the grassy area east of the inn. It was a novelty, but not profitable.

Andrew was known as a good shot and people would throw coins in the air for him to hit with his .22 rifle. They had an interesting souvenir if they could find the coin.

In 1947 or 1948 Andrew and Madge Stewart sold the business to Andy and Pauline Kennedy and Pauline's brother, for $10,000.

Braddock Inn, 1940's

Earl, Audrey and Carl Smith, 1947, new Fort Necessity sign.

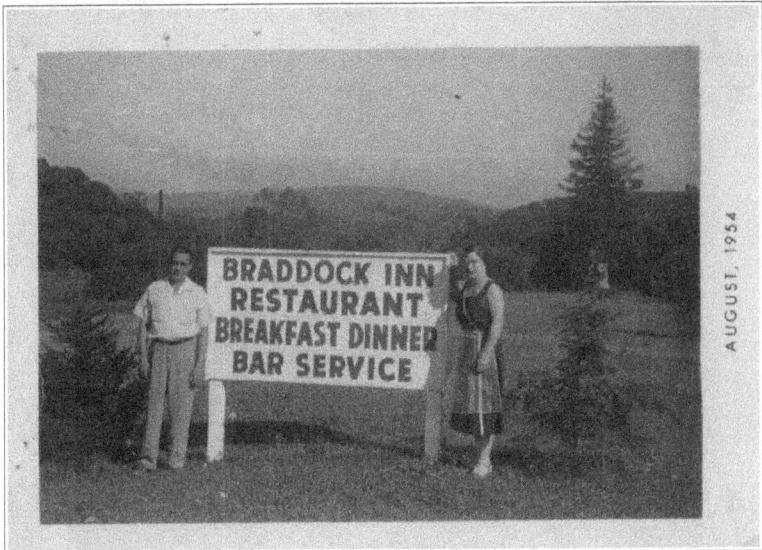

New sign for Andy and Pauline Kennedy, owners of
Braddock's Inn, 1954. The gas pumps were removed.

Frankhouser Clan Holds Annual Event

Frankhouser clan held its annual reunion Sunday at Braddock's Inn.

Officers elected for the coming year include: president, Oliver Frankhouser; vice president, Robert Frankhouser; secretary-treasurer, Helen Marie Newcomer; assistant secretary, Jean Blackburn.

Mrs. Laura Frankhouser, of Uniontown, was the oldest person present and Edwina Jay Walters, daughter of Mr. and Mrs. Edward Walters, also of Uniontown, was the youngest present. Mr. and Mrs. Woodrow W. Frankhouser and son, Edward, of Kent, Ohio, traveled the farthest.

Next reunion of the group will be held the third Sunday in August of 1954 at Braddock's Inn.

Those attending were Mr. and Mrs. Oliver Frankhouser, Mr. and Mrs. Robert Frankhouser, Mr. and Mrs. Ewing Dawson, Mr. and Mrs. Glenn Langley, Allen and Marcha Langley, Mr. and Mrs. Earl Holland, Virginia Holland, John L. Williams, Mr. and Mrs. Russell Newcomer, Mr. and Mrs. Albert Sickles, James and Robert Sickles, Carole and Joyce Ann Sickles, Mrs. Lida Yauger, Harry and Barbara Lou Yauger, Betty Denty, Mrs. Edward Sickles, Mr. and Mrs. Jack Fisher, Jay and Larry Fisher, Bruce and Mary Dorothy Fisher, Mr. and Mrs. Wilbur Cook, Cynthia Cook, Mr. and Mrs. Henry Frankhouser, Rita Frankhouser, John Abdor, Mr. and Mrs. Edward Walters and children, Linda Sue, Bonnie and Edwina Jay; Mrs. Laura Frankhouser, Mrs. Ellen Leighly, Mrs. Ethel Franks, Mr. and Mrs. J. L. Newcomer, Pauline and Emily Newcomer, Martha and Jack Newcomer, Mr. and Mrs. Charles Yauger and children, Frances, Donald, Roberta and Rebecca; Mrs. John Pease, Joan and Janet Pease, Mrs. Jean Blackburn, Janet and Elaine Blackburn, Mr. and Mrs. Glenn Williams, Glenna Williams, Mr. and Mrs. Ernest Everly, Mrs. Grace Fearer, Mrs. Emma Beatty, Mr. and Mrs. William L. Wilyard, Brandonville, W. Va.; Mr. and Mrs. Lloyd Miller and children Dorothea and Jackie, Albright, W. Va.; Mr. and Mrs. R. R. Frankhouser, Brandonville, W. Va.; Mr. and Mrs. William King, Glassport; Mrs. Cora Everly Brandonville, W. Va.; Mr. and Mrs. Ray Frankhouser and children Gerry and Jean, Brandonville, W. Va.; Mrs. Muriel Frankhouser, Albright, W. Va.; Mrs. Ralph Frankhouser, Morgantown, W. Va.; Mr. and Mrs. Dennis Hurley, Pittsburgh; Mrs. Blanche Liston, Terra Alta, W. Va.; Mr. and Mrs. Woodrow W. Frankhouser and son Edward, Kent, O.; Mr. and Mrs. J. C. Church, Bruceton Mills, W. Va.

* * *

PLEASE DRIVE CAREFULLY!

A 1953 reunion at Braddock's Inn.

40

New Room To Open At Braddock Inn

The new Braddock Room of the Braddock Inn on Rt. 40 East near Braddock's Grave will be open to the public on Sunday.

The new room will have facilities for 75 guests.

Mr. and Mrs. Andrew Kennedy, the owners, revealed today that they will cater to bridge parties, private parties, and bowling banquets. They will also serve on the lawn.

The Kennedys operated Paulines' Lunch in the Second National Bank Bldg. arcade for 15 years before acquiring the mountain inn about eight years ago.

New party room added in 1955.

In 1959, a skunk visited Braddock's Inn...

This Skunk Is Skunked At Own Game

Loud thumping noises and barking dogs at 3 a. m. yesterday sent Pauline and Andrew Kennedy, owners of Braddock's Inn, scurrying to investigate.

At the first frightful sounds, Andy hastily donned apparel, grabbed a pistol, turned on all the lights and set out to find the source. However, all became quiet and seeing nothing, he returned to the house.

Shortly later, bedlam broke loose again. Joined by his wife, Andy sallied forth. Their torchlight revealed a full-grown skunk, his head inside a large pickle jar, bumping the wall or driveway with every step and circled by two wildly barking dogs.

Three hours later, still held captive, the animal fell down a coal chute under the house. One hour later, a bread delivery man arrived and offered his help. After a "consultation," Anly and the volunteer helper pushed a long clothesline prop into the coal bin and smashed the jar.

A rope ladder was lowered and when the black and white animal recovered from shock, he climbed his way to freedom.

Then came the sixties...

1961

1966

Braddock Inn, 1970

The 1970's postcard has this information on the back:

Braddock Inn Restaurant, U. S. Rt. 40, 9 miles east of Uniontown, Farmington, Penna., at site of General Braddock's grave and monument.

Specializing in Home Cooked Meals; Cocktail Bar, Picnic Area.

Phone 412 – 329-5508. Pauline Kennedy, Prop.

Great Meadows Garden Club

Christmas Party, 1966, Braddock Inn

Seated L-R: Pauline Kennedy (Braddock Inn owner), Flo
John, Dorthea McGee, unknown, unknown, unknown,
Vivian Guiererre, unknown, unknown, Nancy Sproul,
Margaret George.
Standing L-R: Pat Americo, Audrey Smith, unknown,
unknown, Millie McMullen, unknown, unknown, Ruth
Martin, Lois Thompson, unknown, unknown, unknown,
Ruth Eberly..

Lunch cost $1.75 this day.

AWARD WINNERS — Admiring an artistic arrangement exhibited in the mini-flower show held by the Great Meadows Garden Club at Braddock's Inn are from left, Mrs. Fred Sproul Jr., Award of Horticulture Excellence and Mrs. Joseph Shelby, Silver Education-Conservation State Award. Mrs. J. A. Hewitt received the Special Recognition State Award, Artistic Division. (Herald-Standard Photo)

Winners For Show

Great Meadows Garden Club has announced winners in the mini-flower show held at Braddock's Inn in Farmington.

The special award in the artistic division went to Mrs. J. A. Hewitt for "Mechanicsburg, Pa." The horticulture excellence award went to Mrs. Fred Sproul Jr., for her display of Prince Hendricks Clematis. A state educational award for her exhibit, Pennsylvania Conservation and Protected plants went to Mrs. Joseph Shelby.

Other winners were:

Artistic Division:

Class 1, Alaska, Mrs. France George, first; Portugal, Mrs. Orville Eberly, second; Carmel, Mrs. Robert Fulton, third; Jerusalem Mrs. Philip Jones, H. M.; Class 2, Mechanicsburg, Pa. Mrs. Hewitt, first; New York City, Mrs. George, second; Italy, Mrs. Orville Eberly, third; Mexico, Mrs. Debby Moore, H. M.; Class 3, Paris,

Mrs. Shelby, first; Williamsburg, Mrs. Bea Kaercher, second; Spain, Mrs. Fulton, third; New Geneva, Mrs. A. M. Kovar, H. M.

Class 4, Daisytown, Mrs. Kenneth Minerd, first; Mexico, Mrs. William Merryman, second; Germany, Mrs. Robert Walsh, third; France, Mrs. William Magee, H. M.

Class 5, Haiti, Mrs. Richard Miller, first; Scotland, Mrs. Carl Smith, second; Ireland, Mrs. Vincent Ross, third; Japan, Mrs. Magee, H. M.; North Pole, Mrs. Peter America, H. M.

Horticulture Division:

Class 1, Dutch Iris, Mrs. A. J. McMullen, first; any other iris, Mrs. George, first; Class 2, Lilies (Hermicallis), Mrs. George, first; Mrs. Harvey Thompson, second; Mrs. Nancy Hewitt, third

Class 4, Climbing Rose, Mrs. Shelby, first; floribunda, Mrs. Eberly, first; Mrs. Shelby, third; hybrid tea, Mrs. McMullen, first; peace, Mrs. Lois Thompson,

second; any other rose, Mrs. Mary Shoemaker, first; Mrs. George, third.

Class 5, Perennials: Delphinium, Mrs. Sproul, first; Mrs. McMullen, second; Clematis, Mrs. Sproul, first; Mrs. Eberly, second; Mrs. McMullen, second; Yarrow, Mrs. Eberly, first; Mrs. Fulton, second. Mrs. George, third; any other perennial, Mrs. Fulton, first; Mrs. Eberly, second.

Class 6, annuals: petunia, Mrs. Sproul, first; Mrs. Minerd, second; marigold, Mrs. Fulton, first.

Class 7, Potted Plants, cut gardenia, Mrs. Walsh, first; Pick A Back, Mrs. Merryman, third; collection, Mrs. Eberly, second; Class 8, flowering shrub branch, Mrs. Robert Fulton, first. Class 9, any biennial, Mrs. Shoemaker, first.

Education Division:

Pennsylvania Conservation-Protected Plants and Information. Mrs. Shelby, silver award

Great Meadows Garden Club Officers: Seated L-R: Audrey Smith, Flo John, Nancy Sproul.
Standing L-R: Mary Campbell and Dorthea McGee. Late 1960's meeting at Braddock Inn.

Garden Club Meet

Great Meadows Garden Club met at the home of Mrs. Vincent T. Ross, Deer Lake for lunch and a meeting.

The program was 'Collecting and Preserving Dried Flowers' with Mrs. Peter Americo as speaker. The exhibit was moss arrangement for the parlor with Bea Kaerchner as exhibitor.

The club will have a bake and plant sale at Braddock's Inn Friday between the hours of 1 and 5 p.m.

The horticulture exhibits were: wild snapdragon, Jean Hoover, red ribbon; hibiscus, Jean Hoover, red ribbon; avocado, Charlotte Ross, blue ribbon; dahlia, Mary Shoemaker, blue ribbon; gloriosa daisy, Mary Shoemaker, blue ribbon; gladiola, Mary Shoemaker, blue ribbon; pansy, Madeline Pearsall, red ribbon; hardy aster, Ruth Martin, blue ribbon; celosia, Pat Americo, red ribbon.

1977

48

For The Loveliest Wedding Of The Year

include us in your Wedding Plans

We'll prepare a lovely and delicious Wedding Dinner with all the trimmings in our beautiful spacious dining room. Wide choice of menus, all reasonably priced.

WE ALSO CATER To BANQUETS PARTIES ANNIVERSARIES BUSINESS MEETINGS CLUBS and CHURCHES

YOUR FAVORITE BEVERAGES AT OUR BAR

If you haven't stopped at the BRADDOCK INN, do so, especially during this Bicentennial Year. Delicious home cooked meals in a pleasant wholesome atmosphere.

OPEN DAILY INCLUDING SUNDAY

BRADDOCK INN RESTAURANT

RT. 40—9 MILES E. OF UNIONTOWN—329-5508

1976

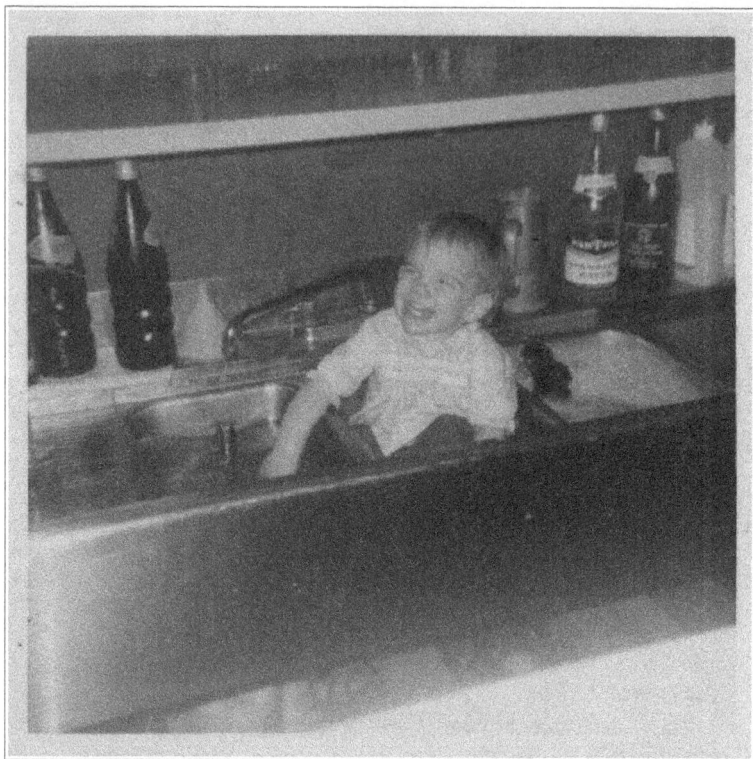

Braddock's Inn tavern sink. Heather Moore Margroff, 1971.

ANTIQUE FLEA MARKET - 1-day, rain or shine, at Braddock Inn. Rt. 40, 8 miles east of Uniontown. Saturday, Sept. 3. For information, call 412-329-4012. s-2

1977.

   In the 1970's, the famous Braddock Flea Markets began and are still a mainstay. The Dunham family were also known for their buckwheat cakes for several decades.

Braddock Inn Today

Twenty years ago, in 1996, Rhonda and Fred Zeigler embarked on a new journey. They purchased the historical Stone House Restaurant from the infamous Fannie Ross. In 2022, the original part of the Stone House Inn will be 200 years old. The front was built by George Titlow in 1909.

With two decades of restauranteur and inn experience under their belts, the Zeiglers have now remodeled the historic Braddock's Inn. These restaurant/inns are within a mile of each other, and both thriving.

I wrote *Stone House Legends & Lore* in 1996. Since then the Stone House has been reborn, and they are working their magic with Braddock's, inn room rentals and all.

Braddock's Inn under construction, Spring 2015.

Braddock's Inn Flea Market, 2015.

Photos on this page by Rich Moel.

Zeigler's remodeled Braddock's Inn on National Pike, 2015.

Braddock's new covered patio entrance, 2016.

Braddock's new patio and bar, 2016.

The Corristan sisters grew up in Ohiopyle. L-R: Roberta Bryner, Nancy Sproul and Beverly Coffman. Their sister, Charlotte Fosbrink left us, regrettably. The "Lunch Bunch" Braddock's Inn, December 2015

Debbie Smith Moore Konechny and Pat Americo (90 years young, Farmington, 2016) chat with the author about old times at Braddock's and the Great Meadows Garden Club.

The new lobby and porch are being added below...

Braddock's Under Construction, 2015...

The new tavern door...

The bar was moved from the front of the restaurant to a cozy corner that leads to the covered patio bar, new kitchen and additional restrooms.

Ralph Coddington, right, and coworker, leveling the floor
for the tavern door, Braddock's, 2015. I have MANY photos
of Ralph through the years, always with a drill or a
hammer!

The front dining room and ice cream parlor.

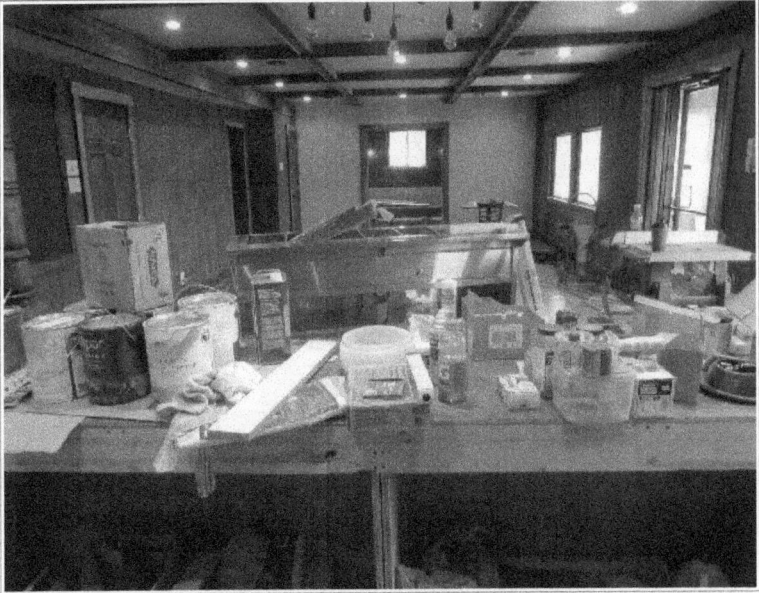

Below, the truck sits where the new covered patio is today.

Both inside and out, the beloved landmark received the overhaul it sorely needed. We are thankful for their country cooking, the new patio and kitchen, the event venue, fun times, inn rooms, and many laughs. *Photo by Rich Moel*

Preparing for the new ice cream parlor and porch.
West side of Braddocks. The back has been extended, adding
a new kitchen and covered indoor/outdoor patio and bar.

Mason Zeigler and the Z team are making their mark on
dirt tracks around the country. www.Masonzeigler.com.

Southwestern PA Slang

Just for fun, I asked friends for their sayings...

Read up your room!

Got a gum band?

Youn's ain't going today.

Just keeping the oars in the water. (Fred Z.)

It's like buying a pig in a poke.

He's a paper devil!

Every day above ground is a good one.

The hurrier I go, the behinder I get.

I am going to the crick!

Ohiopyle's Booism: Wa Wa Buddy!

Thirty couple, twenty couple.

Don't mean me no never-mind!

Picksburgh, PA

We call Pennsylvania, P. A.

Yinz being have?

You can't get there from here...as the first phrase in giving directions from Ohiopyle, PA.

It is much shorter as the crow flies.

Corn will be knee high by the fourth of July.

Lord willing and the creek don't rise.

Not my monkey, not my circus.

That is all caddywhoppus!

You heard me warble!

Nah uh?

Ya huh!

Knee high to a grasshopper

She's crazier than a bessie bug!

Worsh the clothes!

Up 'ere

'tatta mash

Prit near

...of an evening.

Get out of light!

Put some Anchor Hocking in that hole.

Your a-- would be hot too if you just got off the stove.

It won't rain if there is enough blue to make a Dutchman a pair of pants.

Put the tators in the poke.

Comere.

Put the youngins to bed.

You make your bed, you lie in it.

Howpow (for Ohiopyle)

Errand the clothes (ironed).

Let's go to Pechin!

Raining cow sh.. and bricks to splash it.

Slippery as snot on the pump handle!

Closer than fuzz on a tick's ear.

Useless as teats on a boar hog.

Pocat Holler

That's like bear hunting with a switch.

Hain't goinna happin.

Don't be so nebby!

Don't forget to put on your babushka.

Goin' to git some beer.

I might have been born at night, but it wasn't last night.

Jagger bushes.

Weiner roast.

How 'bout dem Picksburg Stillers?

How 'bout dem Buccos?

Youns goin' to Gabes?

Finer than a feather on a frog's front foot!

Rainin cats n dogs...I just stepped in a poodle.

I wretched my back.

I got a hankerin' to...

That's harder than sandpapering a wildcat's a--.

South of 70

Fayettenam

Hoagie

Pop

Chipped Ham

Halushki

If it ain't broke, don't break it.

The bed is mussed up.

I wretched in the cupboard.

Brown paper poke.

I am going to see a man about a dead horse.

How far is it? "Fifteen minutes."

I am so hungry I could eat the south end of a north bound pole cat.

Dippy eggs!

I'll give you somethin' to cry about!

Go cut me a switch for your woopin".

Let's go cow tippin' at Benzio's farm!

I drive a shivy.

I was the first hog at the trough.

If your friends jump off the bridge, would you?

As cute as a bug's ear!

Poke me up a six-pack!

A BIG THANK YOU TO SW PA Sayings Contributors:

Jordan Zeigler DeGusipe, Barbara Androstic, Dave McKnight, Joe McKnight, Odd Phedaque, Lonna Miller, Skeeter McCoy, Brandon Grimm, Patti Pilato, Linda Forquer-Fox, Kathy Sedlock, Bob Hobbs, Cheryl Lane Thomas, Judy Caringola Watson, Joe Cockrell, Billie Myers, Dawn Nicholson Behunin, Sharon Daniels, Greg Mellinger, Sue Moore, Jim Oglethorpe, Debbie Konechny, Kari Kovach Horowitz, Charlie Darr, Charlotte and Clay Fosbrink, Bill Askin, Scott Wagner, Miriam Ofsanik, Betty Moore, Parthena Rodriguez, Jill Harris, Ron Enos, Mel Minnick, Jr. Joey Liston, Kim Patterson, Lonna Miller, Andrew J. Stewart and Cindy Biller.

A HUGE THANK YOU TO MY SPONSORS
ON THE FOLLOWING PAGES...

Restaurant

THE HISTORIC STONE HOUSE EST. 1822
Restaurant • Inn • Tavern

Weekly Restaurant Specials

Monday
  Wing Night
Tuesday
  AYCE Pasta Night
Wednesday
  AYCE Crab Legs Night
Thursday
  Steak Night
Friday-Sunday
  Chef's Features

Restaurant Hours
  Vary by Season
  Call Us For Our Current
  Hours of Operations
  Private Dining
  Available

21 Craft Beers on Tap!
  Enjoy your favorite or
  try something new!

Existing since 1822 gives us a history that not many current dining locations can match. Dine where business magnates, famous politicians and thousands of travelers have enjoyed great food and great service for over 194 years!

Chef Jeremy Critchfield has over 20 years of experience in the kitchens of five star resorts and restaurants all over the country. Chef and his team will thrill your taste buds and exceed your expectations. Our Professional Services Staff will make your dining experience a memorable one!

BUY OUR SAUCES, MIXES AND RUBS!

WWW.STONEHOUSEINN.COM | 724-329-8876

The Historic Stone House | 3023 National Pike | Farmington PA

Backyard Gardens, Ohiopyle

Locally Grown and Locally Made Market.

Open 7 days a week April through mid October,

Weekends through Christmas.

1 Block East of Ohiopyle Falls, Lincoln Street.

Oddly Enough, Ohiopyle

Fair Trade Clothing and Gifts

1 Block East of Ohiopyle Falls, Lincoln Street.

Oddlyenough.biz. The author sports her dress on the back cover.

Michael Lake is now 15 and has taken the checkered flag in the Late and Super Late Model Divisions eight times! Go Michael!

78

Jazz Great, Harold Betters, 88

Betters rocks the Christian W. Klay Winery in
Chalk Hill, August 2016. Three horns, several
singers and a drummer (his grandson, Patrick)
joined in with the band on a day we will always
remember. Thanks, Boss!

AND Sharon, the wine (Nemacolin) was great, too.

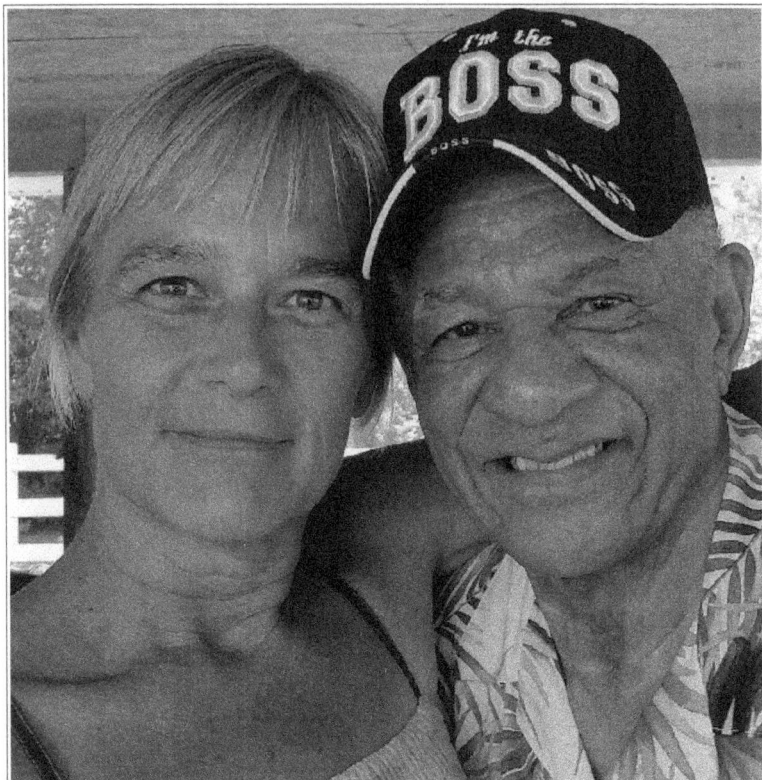

Author Marci Lynn McGuinness and the BOSS, Harold Betters,
C.W. Klay Winery, August 2016.The crowd danced all day.

Marci Lynn McGuinness
Makes History

About the Author:

Marci Lynn McGuinness is a high-energy self publisher whose niche is preserving the remarkable and unique history of Southwestern Pennsylvania. Since 1981, she has written, released and promoted 36 books.

To research her popular 6-book Yesteryear series, she interviewed the culturally rich mountain region's eldest people, recording their memories. The pictorial books relay these stories and those of the thousand vintage photographs she has collected.

McGuinness' work has led her to uncover local history of national significance that only she has published. Two of her books, *Yesteryear at the Uniontown Speedway* and *The Mystery of the Ohiopyle Hotel* are incredible true stories she is adapting to film. From George Washington to General Braddock, silent film stars to the Chevrolet and Duesenberg brothers, McGuinness has discovered untold tales.

The author/screenwriter/historian is the mother of identical twin daughters. She lives near Ohiopyle, Pennsylvania and strives to share the area's exciting legends while playing with her grandson and traveling.

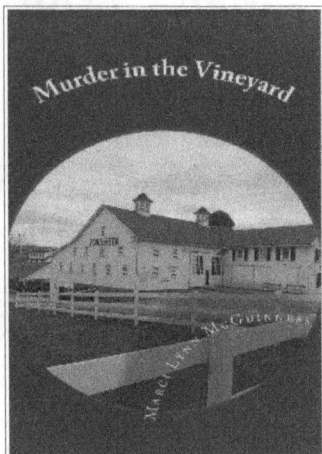

More Books by Marci Lynn McGuinness:

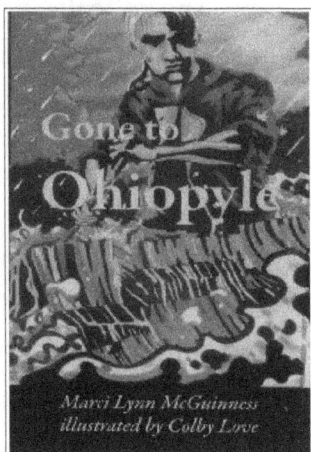

McGuinness' Books, etc...

Laurel Highland Legends, Volume I (2015)

Vivian & the Board Track Boys (2015/e book/story)

The Mystery of the Ohiopyle Hotel (2015 e book/story)

Murder in the Vineyard (2014)

Pam's Cooking (with Pam Bendishaw – 2013)

1915 Uniontown "Summit Mountain" Hill Climb Program Reprint

Murder in St. Michaels (4/2013)

Ohiopyle, That Little Town, WWII (w/ McCahan, 2012)

Speedway Kings of SW PA, 100 Years of Racing History (2011)

Yesteryear at the Uniontown Speedway (1996, 1997, 2008)

Official Program U.S.A. Speedway, 1916 Reprint (1996, 2009)

Message of the Sacred Buffalo (June 2010)

Hauntings Of Pittsburgh & the Laurel Highlands (October 2009)

Gone to Ohiopyle (September 2009)

Murder in Ohiopyle & Other Incidents (Summer 2009)

Butch's Smack Your Lips BBQ Cookbook, (Spring 2009)

Yesteryear in Ohiopyle, Vol. III (2008)

How to be a Working Author/Writer (2005; 2nd Edition, 2008)

Chesapeake Bay Blue Crabs (2004)

In it to Win It (2001)

The Explorer's Guide to the Youghiogheny River, Ohiopyle and SW PA Villages (2000)

Along the Baltimore & Ohio Railroad, from Cumberland to Uniontown (1998)

Stone House Legends & Lore (1998)

Yesteryear in Smithfield (1996)

Yesteryear in Masontown (1994)

Yesteryear in Ohiopyle, Volume II (1994)

Yesteryear in Ohiopyle, Volume I (1993)

No Outlet! (1993)

Incidents (1992)

Nanny's Kitchen Cookbook (1991)

Natural Remedies, Recipes & Realities (1986)

The Deerhunter's Guide to Success (1985)

Natural Remedies (1984)

Unforgettable Poems for Everyday People (1984)

What's Happenin' Around Ohiopyle (1981)

More Publications by McGuinness

Around Ohiopyle Map & News July 2009-2011

Around Ohiopyle Magazine (2008)

Tying the Knot Magazine (2007)

St. Michaels/Tilghman Coupon Booklet (2003-2004)

Yesteryear Calendar series (1990's)

Yesteryear Press (Newsprint Mag.-5 times a year) 1992 – 2002

Speak Easy Digest (Early 1990's-quarterly)

Naturally Yours Newsletter (1980's)

Movies/Scripts

Speed Kings screenplay based on *Yesteryear at the Uniontown Speedway* and *Speedway Kings* books. (2016)

Murder in St. Michaels screenplay (2005)

Yesteryear in Ohiopyle – The Movie (1990's)

McGuinness' books are available on Amazon and Kindle AND at these SW PA shops:

Appalachian Creativity Center, Crawford Ave., Connellsville, PA

Backyard Gardens, Lincoln Street, Ohiopyle, PA

Braddock's Inn, Farmington

Christian Klay Winery, Fayette Springs Rd., Chalk Hill, PA

Pechin Groceries, 119, Dunbar, PA

From Books to Film!

Marci Lynn McGuinness is presently pitching her feature film, *Speed Kings*, to producers. The screenplay is inspired by the characters in her popular books, *Yesteryear at the Uniontown Speedway* and *Speedway Kings of SW PA, 100 Years of Racing History*.

McGuinness, an author/screenwriter/historian, owns the rights to many true stories. Her current projects are a screenplay, *The Mystery of the Ohiopyle Hotel*, a documentary, *Speedway Kings*, and her 37th book, *Laurel Highland Legends*, Volume II.

She is an alumni of Sherwood Oaks Film School and ScreenwritingU of Hollywood, CA.

www.ohiopyle.info

shorepublications@yahoo.com

www.facebook/LaurelHighlandLegends

McGuinness' 36 books are available
on Amazon and Kindle.
www.ohiopyle.info

www.ingramcontent.com/pod-product-compliance
Lightning Source LLC
Chambersburg PA
CBHW031329040426
42443CB00005B/265